AM I REALLY IMPORTANT?
Talk Therapy
ANGEL-CLARE LINTON

am i really important?
Talk Therapy
a poetry collection by angel-clare adiel linton

TALK THERAPY
Copyright © 2023 by Angel-Clare Linton

All rights reserved. No part of this publication may be used in any form or fashion, such as being transmitted or reproduced electronically or physically / mechanically (i.e. recording, photocopying, or any information retrieval and storage system). The writer or publisher must grant written permission unless small portions of this publication are used in reference to critical articles or reviews. Additionally, all names used in this collection are from the poet's imagination. For more information, please visit: www.lintonpress.ca

Cover design and edited by Angel-Clare Linton

ISBN: 978-1-7387049-9-6 (Paperback)
ISBN: 978-1-998214-01-3 (PDF)
ISBN: 978-1-998214-00-6 (eBook)

First edition: December 2023

10 9 8 7 6 5 4 3 2 1

TRIGGER WARNINGS

Talk Therapy is a poetry collection that discusses heavy topics such as depression, suicide, and cutting. Reader discretion is advised.

"The LORD *is* my light and my salvation; Whom shall I fear? The LORD *is* the strength of my life; Of whom shall I be afraid?"
Psalm 27:1 NKJV

TABLE OF CONTENTS

01	Part I - The Whispers in the Dark
65	Part II - The Serpent in the Grave
117	About the Poet
119	Other Books by the Poet

Part I
The Whispers in the Dark

I thought I was doing better. I guess it *was* just an illusion.

how to tell it's time to begin another poetry collection

There are words that whisper,
      float,
            and squishes
the crevasses of my mind
as a tiny and muddy creek
escapes from my dark brown eyes
as the night kisses my cheek.

At first, it isn't a black monster
hiding in my pink brain's attic,
desperate to force my newly bought blade
into my thigh as it would tell me,
"You can stop whenever you want to."

It's the thing that tells me that
I am alone and no one
would understand what

I'm going through,

as if that thing wants to isolate me
from the speech bubbles

that bounce outside of my body.

"You can stop whenever you want to."

There's this silence in my room
with anticipation of my life
shattering as if I was walking
on the highway at 1:03 a.m.
with my feet kissing the ground,
desperate to escape
from the needles
and broken shards of glass.

It's standing at the edge of the bridge,
looking down and wondering,
is this what it feels like to almost die?

cutting is

like seeing the stars in the middle of the night as you drive home from your evening class because it was the only time slot available, and you want to graduate in the Spring.

being in control of the tiniest grey goo while rockets are crashing around your house. The tiniest grey goo swishes around your hand, desperate to turn black and join its kind.

the silver blade hidden in my closet, dancing in the box that it was bought in.

an itch in therapy that floats in the back of my head as a river slowly streams down my face. *I am alone.*

the silver metal that wraps around my body in the middle of the night, whispering, stringing me on to want to dance with it in the bathroom lighting.

the open wound on my thigh, stinging whenever I lay in bed, trying to sleep on my queen-sized bed as I twist and turn as frosty blue ice hits my body.

distress cries in the distance as it bounces off the ocean's sparkling water.

a band-aid getting ripped off an open wound on my thigh.

the whisper in the night.

"stop"
"never"

"You can stop whenever you want."
"You're in control."
      "I gotta make sure to pace myself."
       "I can't let other people know."
         "I'm in control."
"You've managed to not do it for this long."
"Please, don't feel guilty."
"Please don't give up."
       "I can't let anyone know."
"You'll be alright."
"You don't even have to cut deep."
        "People wouldn't care."
  "I promise you, you'll be alright."

i was going to kill myself.

It was the middle of the afternoon,
and I was sitting on my bed
with my laptop in front of me.
My light pink walls
that were painted years ago
shun around me like a star
glistening in the night sky
during the winter. My clothes
were piling up on my chair,
tall enough to be considered a mountain
for people to climb up
and ski or snowboard down
as if they were on a school field trip.

        2 p.m. on June 23rd, 2023.
Counselling should be starting now.

The sun was trying to make its way
through my thick curtains, trying
to peer in to see what items
it could shine on.

                    2:01 p.m.
He's here.
My heart was skipping in my chest
and beating in my ears
like a car starting first thing in the morning.

It was like the sun and the moon
clashed with each other
in the middle of the day
during the winter as they fought
to see which could haunt
the people underneath them
like a sea monster.

              I was going to kill myself.
I wanted to flush myself out of this world,
        desperate
to remove this thick black monster
from my shoulders that more or less
        constantly
weighed me down
like someone being carried on my back.

Saturday was trying
to obtain my reach, whispering,
"Today would be the perfect day.

Please believe me."

                    Suicide.

You should kill yourself.

No one would miss you.

You should do it.

"What can you do to remain safe?"

The silence was chirping
like the silence
in the middle of the night,
hungry for something to happen.

He sits in silence with me.

We booked another session
for Monday because
      I promised
to see him soon, meaning that
I can't break it.

I didn't break that promise.

the 6 o'clock shadow

The sun shimmers at 6 in the evening.
The children laugh
on the basketball court down the street.
The half-moon is halfway in the baby blue sky
as it whispers at the sun, desperate
to meet it again.
The black crows with a white line
coating their back circles the skies.
The dark green leaves dance with each other.
The window in the kitchen is open as

the man and woman sway together,

dancing hand in hand
like they were at prom again
as they take to the dance floor
while the silver disco ball
      bounces
off the black ceilings.

Her black hair's tied up in a bun
with tiny pieces flopping above her forehead.

The grassy field
        sways
with the whitely transparent wind
        as it tries
to be filled
with red and yellow flowers.

Children dance in the sprinklers
as their feet sink into the Earth.

Joyful happiness loudly whispers in the sky
as if trying to serenade the people on the moon.

                      My heart fights to beat in my chest
                      as it consumes my ears while trying
                          to suffocate me by my throat.

                            My legs shake
                      as if they don't belong to
                my body anymore.
                          They quiver and cry
                like a wounded puppy alone
                    in the thick green forest.

                            My thighs cry out,
                          wanting the sweet
                    kiss of the rainbow
                        floating in the air.

                My thighs want the sweet kiss of red lips
                          as they explore my body,

wiping away the wounds
that constantly cry as they wish
to be opened again.

My body wants to be loved, too.

the monster

This black goo would crawl
over my body,
wanting to come inside
and then pushing
itself into my vessel,
trashing around like a hurricane.
                It was my own hurricane.
The goo made itself a star
as it would leak out from my fingertips,
desperate to be seen as if its endless
hole wasn't already admired,
as if it was a twinkling star
crashing down on Earth.
It would thread its way
into the pages like tattoo ink.

The black goo turned itself
into a poetry collection,
capturing a moment in time
like a photo taken on a DSLR camera.
      It cries out
as if it has been caught in a bear trap.

The goo wanted the yellow-tinted spotlight
to shine onto it like it was a singer
or dancer on the stage of a school's theatre.

Its voice would boom around the walls,
assaulting the ears of people
walking past the auditorium.

                There's this black goo stuck to my back,
             ready to consume me like a hungry cat
                    ready to pounce on its prey
                        in the depths of the forest.
                    It pours onto pure white pages,
       desperate to be seen once again.

counselling notes

- I wanna die, but I'm afraid to pull the trigger.
- It's "funny" how I'm scared to die, but I've attempted more than once.
- Maybe people would enjoy my art after I've died.
- It was even said in that one song.
- Maybe I would be worth more after I'm dead.
- After reading my poetry collection, how do I handle a possible crowd coming at me with fiery pitchforks?
- I'm cutting again.
- Cutting gives me the excuse not to talk to anyone about my feelings.
- How do I learn how to cope without drowning in the thick blue water as it swishes around me like seaweed?
- Want to know the different ways I wanna kill myself?
- Tell him the different ways I want to kill myself because it's helpful for whatever... I think.
- I want to die.

counselling

1. Log in as I sit on my bed with my "phone" in hand with the note-taking app open as my heart rate increases as if I was in high school gym again running the 5k.
2. Watch the time every second as if I was counting down to my birthday.
3. The counselling time hits, and I wonder if he forgot about me.
4. A minute passes, and I check to see if I have the time right.
5. *The host has joined the meeting. We're letting them know you're here.*
6. A couple of seconds later, I'm sitting in front of the screen as the pop-up comes up, letting me choose if I want to connect to the audio now or test my microphone.
7. My heart continues to nearly beat out of my chest as he waits for my audio to be connected before saying "hey" with a smile.
8. Begin flowing my feelings out to him as if I've known him longer than I have.

the dying galaxy

The night was sparkling in the day.

The blue roses were wilting in the ocean.

The sea was walking on the sandy land
as it tried to reach the moon,
wanting to stay with her forever.

The stars do not exist.

The skies refuse to sparkle.

The woman at the end of the street
refuses to keep breathing.

      The night begins to dwindle,
     mixing its galaxy into the day
    like an alphabet soup, desperate
      to remain alive like me.

The day mixes and tries to dance.
It doesn't wanna die.

The waterfalls are drying.

The dark blue oceans
are getting tinted black
while the ground is slowly
turning grey,
matching the grey-tinted air
that has long since formed.

I want to die.

I don't wanna die.
                         Please don't let me die.

hatred

While the clouds
were covering the sparkling sun,
the white lights
of the bathroom illuminated my frame.
Make sure you slowly
have the blade come onto your skin.
There's nothing to be afraid of.

There's no black monster consuming me.

The trees ain't dying in the corner of my heart.

My mind ain't tinted black
from the monster slushing around
like I'm its permanent home.

The house is silent
as if holding its breath
as it watches me
make a deeper-than-normal cut
on the outside of my left thigh.

Why did you stop there?

The blood bleeds out,
dripping down my leg
like a river in the summer.
It's warm, like a mother's hug
before she puts you to bed.

Using the toilet paper,
I wipe it away
before quickly putting brown band-aids
on the scars as they still slightly bleed.

    Hatred.

The unfinished *h*
lies on my thigh, desperate
to be completed like an unfinished book
sitting on a bookshelf in someone's bedroom.

It's desperate to be flashed out to the world
like a freshly-inked tattoo.

"relapse"

I press the newly bought blade
into my skin as my chest
caves into my heart,
desperate to feel its warmth and hug.
My skin stings as it hums
to the drumming of my heart.
      Thump thump.
           Thump thump.
                Thump thump.
The almost summer sun shines
just outside of the house,

                                  my house,

desperate to get its yellow rays
into my bones and ingraining those rays
into the stems of my brain.

The blade accidentally
lightly slices the top
of my ring finger on my right hand.
Blood pools on the finger
before running down my hand and palm
before slightly tinting the countertop.

    Thump thump.
           Thump thump.
                    Thump thump.
The open wound
is like an injured black cat
abandoned at the side of the highway
I've wanted to jump off of.

It lightly hisses under the band-aid,
wanting to escape from my thigh
and from being "just another scar."
    Thump.
        Thump.
                Thump.

my introduction

I'm very new here and don't know what else to do or where to go.

It's like I'm drowning in this black ocean at the end of the world, and the only way I can cope is by pouring my words into a separate ocean called "poetry" and on my skin. Suicide is bouncing off the walls of my black goo mind more and more.

I try to smell the pink flowers floating through my imagination and hold onto them like a hot air balloon, ready to take me to another nation.

I don't know what to do while the night is sparkling throughout the country as I lay on my bed, watching videos on my laptop as my fingers fly across the keyboard, desperately wanting the galaxy of inky words to be engraved on the screen.
There's the comfort in pouring my tears onto the page and releasing it to the world, capturing my life as if I'm a videographer or photographer at my own wedding that I dreamed about when I was younger.

I don't know who to talk to.

I don't know who to trust.

i've tricked him, too

I scrunch my nose
whenever pink words flow
from his lips as he sits
on the other side of the screen.
His background is blurred
like my vision whenever tears
consume my eyes
in the middle of the night
or whenever I read anything
without my glasses, and part of me
wants to strain my eyes,
but the larger part of me doesn't,
refusing to have my eyes work overtime.

> It's as if a large
> part of my brain
> doesn't comprehend
> what to do
> when
> someone outside
> my immediate family
> decides to throw me a compliment.

Should I throw it into the ocean
and watch it drown
as the imaginary hands wave
above the raging sea,
or should I hold it
and keep it in my back pocket
so that one day, when the sun is setting,
I can take it out
and pretend that everything
is okay, even if it's just for a second?

Apparently, I am smart and creative
      (according to *them*),
and they dwell someplace in my mind.
Or maybe it's better
to say that it *hides*
somewhere in my mind
and only comes out
in the middle of the night
or when I sit in front of my computer
in my university classroom,
slowly having an internal meltdown
as I stare at the questions
of the midterm or quiz,
slightly sweating
as a ball of worry
coated in matte ice blue
nearly consumes my body.

I should throw the compliment
in the beach's ocean

>   *before turning my back*
>   *and walking back to the bus stop,*
>   *hoping that I find the bus stop that I need*
>   *and praying that the one that I stumble across*
>   *will come within 20 minutes.*

"I ain't smart or creative," I say
as I look out at the distance
as if I'm a teenager again
looking through the window,
acting like those teenagers in movies.
"And I can just *feel*
a compliment coming," I say, smiling.
He laughs, his smile covering his entire face,
and my smile grows.

the emptiness
of the night lingers over me

I don't know where to go
when the night
is settling in my mind
as it travels down to my body,
trickling between my fingers
and the veins that nearly protrude
out of the top of my hands
as they haunt the slushy world.

                    My mind is a broken record
                    stuck on two or three songs
                    on its debut sad rap album
                as it sings on the loudest volume
                      in an abandoned building
                      next to the secondary school.

                          I'm alone in my room
                    as my laptop screen shines
                    on my face like the sun,
                    trying to provide comfort
          like a friend
                who claims to be there for you.

The scattered alphabet
swarms around me
with its warmth as their words
lightly implant themselves on my body
as they tell me,
"We're always here for you"
and
"You can trust us."

Like stamps,

they mark me

with a temporary tattoo
while insisting
on making it permanent.
"Please don't leave us."

"We need each other."
"You can't live without us,

and you know it."

I don't know where to go
when the day shimmers
outside of my mind
as it seeps out of my brain,
creating a puddle
that appears much
shallow than it is.

I don't know what to do
when my blood seeps out,
insisting that it's better
to be outside of me
than forced to be in a body
that already doesn't want it.

I don't know what to do
when the silence consumes body,
holding my wrists on my bed.

        "Get me out of here."

Sometimes, when the sun
        is melting, and the moon is crashing,
            I fantasize about how effortless
it would be to cut myself
        in the bathroom and bleed out.
The air would be coated in the stars

        from the galaxy.
           I would hold my breath,

        scared that if I were to breathe,
I would cut deeper than necessary

or would mess up the cut somehow.

The waves keep moving,
    pushing closer and closer
to the hand holding the blade.

    The hand presses deeper and deeper.
At least deeper than usual.

        What do I do
when my hand begins to falter,
    and the blood continues
to seep out from my skin?

          Help me.

the world doesn't lose its shimmer

The world was still moving
on its axis when I was determined
to kill myself in October.

*Even I can't escape
the clichés and the poetry
about the darkened days in October,
the fall blues, and the world
still moving on its axis.*

I'm alone.
*Those words bounced
throughout my body, reminding me*

I would not be missed when I die.

The hospital walls,
with how ugly the paint was
and how stale and quiet the room was,
was enough of a cause
to want to kill myself even more.

The mental health section

of the hospital was quiet,
almost itching and begging people
to lose their minds
as they were forced to sit and linger
with their thoughts.
Killing myself would have been better
than sitting in this room
as the officers wait outside.

        I think the room was just a dumping ground,
        a place people of authority
        were able to place me
        and forget about me as if I was trash
        lying on the streets
        as cars would fly past me
        as they daydream, their heads
        halfway to the moon as the
        swooshing
        noise of the trash
        doesn't register in their mind.

The world continued,
the weight of me wanting
to kill myself never registering.

    Never making a dent

    while the world never falters.

    Do you know what it feels like
    to want to die and people not care?

The waves continued to clash
with one another, playing
as children ran into it,
wanting to play with them, too.

Would you come to my funeral when I die?

Do you know what it feels like
to basically attempt to kill yourself
and people not notice?

Get up.
Read the Bible.
Brush teeth.
Be productive.

                    Get up.
               Read the Bible.
                 Brush teeth.
                Be productive.

                                      Get up.
                             Read the Bible.
                               Brush teeth.
                             Be productive.

Pretend that nothing happened the previous day.

                             Pretend the day before
                                 was just an off day
             like someone who doesn't work on Mondays

and who wanted to relax,
feeling as if working consistently for six days
has put an added emotional weight
consuming the entire body,
only to be washed out
by having at least one day of rest.

My heart continues to beat
in my chest, unaware
of the previous night's events,
still wanting to keep me alive.

The following day,
my body was quiet,
wanting to return
to what was supposed to be normal.

The world is still moving as I contemplated:

Should I attempt again?

failure always eats with me

There's no galaxy floating in my world,
desperate to keep me mixing and floating
through its skies. It also seems
as if "the other side"
doesn't wanna swallow me,
      consuming me
in its unknown milky texture and spice.

"Do you miss me yet?

      Cuz I don't miss you.

You want someone to miss you so badly, huh?"

The world is desperate
to be silent without me,
yet "the other side" desperately
wants me to remain in the world,
telling me, "People would miss you."

"Stop listening to all these lies.

Please listen to me.
*   You've known me longer.*
*   Who are you going to listen to?*
Some stranger or me?"

         Suicide
dances in the corner
with a smirk or a grin
(it seems like it doesn't wanna decide)
as it stares me down,
its all-black eyes blasting through my soul.
It wants me to drop my eyes
as if that's a sign that Suicide has won.

"You can't have me," it whispers,
tempting me to run and cry
like the little girl I used to be.

"Did you think
you would have been able to have me?"

         "You are such a failure."

"You can't do anything right."

"You couldn't even kill yourself properly."

suicide is

the waves in the distance while sitting in your perfect home that's only shown in television shows.

the sun in the background as it sets over the hill.

watching your favourite television show on your laptop as you lay on your bed in the middle of the night after a long day at school.

sleeping in the middle of the day as the sun plays with the beach's sea.

the ring on my middle finger as it glistens in the artificial light.

sitting in a fast food restaurant eating a hamburger while music plays through your matte black headphones as light, "comforting" music plays on the speakers.

the stranger down the road heading toward you. *What if he's trying to kill me?*

the rain raging down as the sun shimmers in the sky.

the prickling red rose bush at the corner of 6th and 7th.

sitting on the porch as children play on the hill in the distance.

the hidden monster in the dark green bush, ready to pounce on its innocent victim.

suicide.

hidden in a sweater and long pants

I started cutting again,
wanting the silver blade
to shine in the bright white light
of the bathroom
while the blade quickly cut across the skin
        on my thighs.
Fresh scars litter my skin,
slowly replacing the old ones.
     You should just cut again.
        No one would notice
           if you made another cut.

You should just cut.

    Cut.   *Cut.*

            Cut.

    Cut.   *Cut.*

There would be a pebble
rolling down the hill,

triggering the continuing rolling of the cuts.

   Cut.   *Cut.*

      Cut.

   Cut.   *Cut.*

My thighs ache for more cuts
to wander throughout them
like young adults wandering
throughout the city
in the middle of the night,
desperate to be at a party.

The first cut
was like permission
for me to make more and
to continue without an itch
of regret pestering
at the back of my mind,
wondering if I had made the right decision.

It's almost as if the fresh air
rejoices whenever it sees me making cut after cut.

   Cut.   *Cut.*

      Cut.

   Cut.   *Cut.*

As my heart
continues to beat
and my mind
continues to wander
in the background,
the urge for my hand
to slash up my skin
after grabbing at the sliver
of reason will continue
to fester at the front of my mind,
eager for me to do it.

      Cut.   *Cut.*

                       Cut.

      Cut.   *Cut.*

an ocean surrounds my heart,

but it doesn't drown me
like the salty ocean
drowning a lake filled with people.

The sky is raging blue,
wanting to force me into a drift-filled hole,
desperate for me to be buried alive.

I sit at the end of the table
in the classroom
as my classmates type away
on their keyboards
or have their pens in their hands
as ink drops onto the pages
of their notebooks made for school,
forming words that are dancing in their headd.

No one here likes me, I think
as the room is filled with muted work.

Maybe I should just disappear.

The silence creeps in the distance.

The sun tries to beam
through the small windows.

A handful of people
walk past the classroom,

sometimes glancing inside the room.

I glance at my classmates

as their heads are knees deep in their writing.

The cold room contradicts
the warmth on the outside.

Someone has someone, except for me.
What *person* do I go to
when the air is tightening around me?

When is a break enough of a break?

When do I make the windshield
stop breaking in?

The ocean surrounds my heart,
slowly eating me from the inside
like a pig eating anything at a pig farm.

The ocean is slowly dying.

the stars are suffocating me

I'm stuck in this well
where the stars in

the galaxy are dying,

and the pictures of me
are fading into the black hole.

Blackness consumes me,
trapping me in its seemingly
endless box as a   one-way mirror
sits somehow perfectly in the middle.

People walk around me,
        sometimes
stopping to stare at themselves
        in the mirror
before crossing the street
in front of them, careful
not to get hit by the cars
that almost always halt to a sudden stop
as if they didn't see the person wanting to cross.

Whenever people
stop to stare at their faces
filled with pores,
I almost always pull back,
desperate to create a galaxy
or an endless black pit in between us.
My knees would be to my chest
with my arms wrapped around them
as if that would help me somehow.

    I want to swallow myself whole,
    desperate to be in the abyss
    as if I was meant to be there.

I want the stars
to overwhelm my brain
as if that would help

wash away the monsters hidden within it.

I want to be something
that doesn't be stared at
from the inside out,
criticizing me like a work of art.

cut and repeat

There used to be more fresh cuts
consuming my thighs
when I was 18 years old. But now,
freshly healing scars are littering
them, some of them covering
the old ones as if it's insulting them.
As if it's payback to my younger self
       somehow.
Now, there are more fresh
scars dancing on my thighs,
trying to hide with the rest
because it takes after me
with wanting to blend in with the crowd,
but knowing it can't
because it'll always stand out.

The cuts heal
like dark purple candy
sunbathing in the middle of the day.
My pants cover the drying scars
as they ache whenever I move
in a semi-awkward position

or whenever I sit down.
It's as if the scars want to be known
by the outside world

as if it's trying to get me professional help.
    They dance
whenever my thighs move
as they suffocate from my own skin
as they try to suffocate me in return
as some form of revenge
like a red slimy monster
forced into the sewage system
because the city kicked it out.
                          They want to wrap
                    their scars around my neck,
                        leaving scratches
                like a thorn-filled rose bush,
            wanting to come for my brain
                and scratch up my mind,
trying to ruin the supposed perfect creation.

            Part of the bigger perfect creation
        lies in my head, not swishing around
            like pebbles in a small fish tank
                  filled with water
           with no fish because it died
only the previous night. *Maybe it would be better*

if my brain bounced around my mind.
        Maybe somehow, it would be better that way.
        Maybe it's better that way.

where is love?

Love is hidden
somewhere outside,
like when I played hiding games
with my friends during the summer
when we were children
and didn't have to worry
about adult responsibilities
or scheduling our entire life
around work and/or school.

The love walks out on me
      when I cry
in the middle of the night,
only to be seen when I'm cutting
in the middle of the day, thinking,
This would be harder than I thought it would be.

                      Love is contained
               in the silver razor blade
                  as it sings to me
           throughout the day, begging
           me to have it kiss my skin.

Love is like a silky light red blanket.

    Love is hidden somewhere.

two days

This would be harder than I thought,
I think as I reset how many days
I've been "sober" from cutting.
  Two days.
The cuts are light, wanting to make sure
that they've been healed
by the time I go to the pool
for my birthday, only to be seen
as a distant memory. *I thought*
I would be able to stop for a month.
I thought I was in control.
I thought I would be able to be in control.
I would watch the blood
s
  l
    o
      w
       l
        y
pour out from my body. The light

from the bathroom would somehow

illuminate the blood even more
as I sat on the toilet.

There was an itch today
when I was sitting in my classroom
as I sat across from her.
    You should just cut.
    You should have walked with your razor.
    You could have been cutting right now.

    I don't know why you didn't think ahead.

I should have had a replacement
in the meantime. I should have
listened to him. *I thought*
I would have been able to manage this on my own.

The cuts linger around my body,
healing and shedding like a dog's fur.
It also whispers,
    You should make more cuts.
     You shouldn't stop cutting.
      You know you need me.

    And maybe I need you, too.

yellow

The sun's in the middle
of the sky as the wind blows
through the rips of my jeans,
my fresh self-harm scars leaking through.
A handful of cars zoom on the street
as the wind continues to whip around me
like a butterfly with painted white wings.

The air doesn't smell
like the brewing forest fires
that *desperately*
consumed as much of the skies
and earth as possible
in the limited time it knew it had.
For a moment, my mind is quiet
as I cut through the hot, lingering air.

Maybe this is what happiness feels like.

appreciate the little things (i)

The mystery hidden under the cabinet.

The sea reaching its invisible border.

The moon haunting the sun
during the thick of summer.

A freshly taken hot shower
an hour before going to bed.

My Bible that I painted
two or so years ago.

The Bible app
that lies on the homepage of my "phone."

Rap music blasting
through the speaker
as I take a hot shower
before going to bed.

The quietness on the public bus.

Cold air blowing while walking
to the bus stop as the sun beats down.

Having enough money
to eat out with my friends
but then immediately wondering,
"Can I financially recover from this?"
as I swipe my debit card
into the machine at the carnival.

A full battery of electronics
before leaving to study
with my friend at the public library
or somewhere on campus.

A clean house.

Not missing the bus
after leaving 6 minutes
later than usual.

Finishing an assignment.

Finding a good book.

Waking up consumed
in a warm home
with other homes surrounding it
with families nearby.

Waking up another day.

my boyfriend,
the green monster

Suicide is like my ex-boyfriend.
Before I met it, I would dance
in the fluffy clouds. My hair
would be tied back,
but the front pieces
would flop around my face
as I twist and turn
while staring at the rainbow
as it continues to cast its promise
throughout the earth-shattering skies.

At some point, though, when my back
was turned, Suicide walked in
as if it knew me from when I
was in secondary school. Suicide
would then slip its arms
around my waist, pulling me close
and whispering its cliché sweet nothings.
Except rather than the sweet nothings
being covered in hot pink and red,
it's tainted dark grey and black,
and it comes out from Suicide's

garbage-smelling breath
as its dancing words whip
its toxic chemicals around me,
      tainting the air.
It forces me closer and closer,

its garbage essence rubbing
off onto me. Its body
squishes onto mine,
and I'm consumed
in its grey texture
and its all-knowing smells,
and my skin radiates
dark grey with black tints.

                                  My clouds are fading,
                               and I'm rapidly falling
                             as the air around me
                    grows tighter and tighter.

Suicide is like my ex-boyfriend
who would want me to
to give him a hand job
as we're in his grey bedroom
in the summer's afternoon
even though I didn't want, to
but I did because
      he was my boyfriend.

Suicide is like a toxic boyfriend
as it (he) walks into the room, demanding
love that I wasn't comfortable with as

his snake eyes
would look up and down my body,
ready to eat me.

Suicide is

the moonlight

It itches.

It dies before waking up and dying again.

It's the nosebleed
in the middle of the hot summer night.

It's the dancing of the sunlight
through the window at 8 p.m.

It's the cold wind in the heatwave.

It's the self-harm scars on my right arm.

It's the calm waves at midnight

     while there's

a white flag waving just above the ocean.

not everything is okay.

I stand in the middle
of the neon yellow crowd,
      screaming
as my black goo gets thicker
while continuing to spread all around my body,
desperate to latch onto *anything*.

The neon yellow crowd
has large, dark purple wings
that occasionally flap around,
exploring the world with child-like wonder.

Neon-yellow people walk around me
as if I'm in a glass cage
in the only zoo in the province.
Grey fear glosses over their eyes
as they side-eye me, careful
to not have their wings   touch me
as if I would pass on a *disease* to them.

They're too scared to touch me,
yet this light blue curiosity

gets the better of them, insisting
they come here to see me.
They're too desperate
to be in the same vicinity as

someone melting.

        You know, not everything is okay.

The sky is slowly turning black,
and the sun no longer comes out
to play in the midst of the day,
causing children to joyfully scream
before they run outside and play.

The stars are white, fighting
to be seen through the heavy mist
of the blackness coating the once-yellow city.

But that's before you say that

        not everything is okay.

You claim that the dark blue rain constantly
falls, splashing down on the cold ground,
desperate to consume you in it.
The dark blue rain
spits black ink like a leaking pen
during the mist of the humid Spring.

        I think things are starting to be okay.

The sun's starting to break through
the thick grey clouds.
The Earth's still somehow spinning on its axis.

The birds are finally chirping
in the light pink air
as they sweep in and out of the trees,
rustling the leaves.

    I think things are starting to be okay.

Part II
The Serpent in the Grave

Please don't tick me, too.

counselling notes

- I don't know if I want to die or if I just want to escape this black goo.
- I'm cutting slightly deeper.
- I think I'm a financial burden.
- I don't like how I can't afford anything.
- I don't think I have any noteworthy accomplishments.
- I think people think I'm more accomplished than I actually am.
- I don't like myself.
- I don't know how I feel about staying alive for other people.
- I'm easily replaceable.
- I don't like myself.

now that i've "relapsed," i feel like there's nothing to live for

Eat. Sleep. Read the Bible.
      Cut.
Work. Pretend I'm okay.
Hang out with family and friends.
      Sometimes, I wonder,
          What is there to live for?
Not in that particular order.

         I want to die.
           I don't wanna die.
      Why am I still here?
         I'm happy I'm still here.

Transparent pink clouds
that *they've* self-titled "emotions" (*sometimes*
masked with vibrant ecstasy)
lie between the thinly veiled spaces
of the razor blade, crying out, *needing*
attention like a lonely young adult
on the dark green and purple playground
discarded like household trash.

What is there to live for?

The thought of *death*
lingers around my head,
sometimes shaking
like something in a bottle
that claims to be magical, with wings
that have fairy stardust mixed all
around the bottle, desperate
to keep *something alive.*

Death swivels in between the features
of the blade, forcing my hand,
wanting to make love to my skin,
wanting to go deeper and deeper,
like digging through trash
as if its hunger has gotten to its breaking point.

I want to die.

I don't wanna die.

Why am I still here?

I'm happy I'm still here.

You should die.

Should I die?

I'm too scared to die.

Eat. Sleep. Read the Bible.
      Cut.
Work. Read the Bible.
Hang out with family and friends.
But not in that particular order.

the fear of losing my friends after graduation

My graduation date
slowly creeps up on me
like the black monster
that always seems to *love*
following me around for what feels
like has been a decade and a half,
but realistically, it has only been nearly 5 years.

    Graduation.

School has   *always*   forced
my time into its hands, conforming me
to its values and making my decisions
without sitting down and talking to me
like a therapist
in my weekly online sessions.

The countdown began
the semester before.
    Next semester will be the last
    summer semester of school ever.
You can dance in the wind

as people are out at a corporate job
as it drains them like a river
being drained during the summer heatwave.

This semester's sunshine beams
through my chest,   nearly
impaling my heart as it tells me,
This is your last summer semester.
         Think about your sparkling future
as you get to dance in the moonlight
while your silver plate gets to be   *slightly*
lighter, like pounds of feathers,
as you get to swim whenever
you want and have your fingers   *fly*
across your keyboard whenever you want.
         Think about it.
Your blocked-out time
wouldn't be etched out so much anymore
like your cuts on your thighs and arms.

         Graduation.

It plays at the back of my mind
like music on the radio
sitting in the kitchen
as the family moves
throughout their home while the time
         ticks
to midnight the following day.
         It plays at the back of my mind
         and creeps forward

whenever I debate
on doing homework first,
writing Talk Therapy, or
editing a manuscript to publish.

Then my plate wouldn't be so full,
like after eating my dinner
on a Saturday evening.

Postgrad.

It's as if it's synonymous
with being friendless
while locked in your room
after you've consumed your life
with work that barely
wants to pay you in the first place.

Friendless.

It's the abyss
as it stares back at me
with dark blue or green puppy dog eyes,
begging me to come with it.

There would be sweet humming
like from a singer practising
right before their concert as it would whisper,
You should just focus on work. Your friends
would be too consumed
with their moving life,

*like them walking on a treadmill
before leaving you, realizing
that they would be better off without you.*

loss

The dark red silk curtain
hiding my body but never
obscuring my face would be draped away,
revealing my failing organs
(but more importantly,
my failing heart and debatably
my mind) when the graduating
class of 2024 would throw our caps
in the air   *just*
before the closing music plays.
We would walk off the stage
before reuniting
with our family and friends.
We would take pictures
          and videos
with one another with smiles
plastered on our faces
while people around us would try to get past us.

In the following few days,
my friends and I
would most likely sit a restaurant in the city

as we celebrate graduating with our
        bachelor's in the arts.
Buzzing from our moderate group
will slowly spread throughout the establishment
while other people bury themselves
in thick velvet conversation,
insisting that   whatever
they're talking about
        is more vital
than the rest of us.

But then that would be the last time
we would ever see (and talk to) each other,
our sweet candy-scented memories
of one another floating in our minds
before they get lost in translation.

And then, who knows.
Maybe one of us
will write a poem about what happened.

painted

Social media is painted in
      red and blue
as people on the other side
of the screen have dark purple tears
leaking from their panda eyes
and dropping like a tiger-sized balloon
as it roars, the sound waves
      echoing
and bouncing off the abyss' walls.

      "Better late than never,"
the text reads
as her "L" is the main focus
of the image, the sun shining
through the screen.

      She has been alive longer than me,
      her breath barely visible
      through the light pollution
      that littered the dark blue skies.

Should I already have my license?

I sit on the bus that
goes to the station,
my school bag on my lap
and my earphones plugged into my

"phone."

On "B's" IByte Story, she documents
      walking into the place
      to take her Learner's test,
      and, what seems like little time passes
      through the magical wonder
      of social media, she comes back,
      beaming with her L in hand.

I wish I had my license already.

      I wish I had more money.

I wish I had my license already.

Driving means

there's the freedom of the open air

as it blasts through the windows,

nearly cracking the glass.

It means that the radio music

would blast throughout *my* car

while my seat would be slightly

higher than usual.

The bus speeds down the road

as if it's three and a half minutes
behind schedule.

Maybe I'm behind schedule.

Maybe I haven't been working hard enough.
                              You should work harder. You should
                                     pour your orange juice
                                 into a bigger cup and extend
                                   yourself into it, trying
to please the cup while keeping yourself sane.

                                How do you expect to be successful
                                  if you aren't spilling yourself
                                    into the cup while trying
                                      to create a galaxy for it?

                    Maybe you should have quit a long time ago.

                           Maybe you should have tried harder
                         the first time you tried to kill yourself.

i just wanna fit in

You should get a job.
    It's weird
        that you aren't working right now.
You're just lazy.
If other people are working
    while in school, then you
        should be able to do it, too.
What are you doing?
    Why are you relaxing?
You're just wasting valuable time.
You should be working harder.

There's this *thing*
hidden deep within my body, lingering
around me less than once a month.
It ain't like a transparent being lurking
in the dark like those monsters
in a sewer system. On a few

selected days, the monster whispers
in my right ear during the middle of the night.

You're a failure.
You should already have a job.
You should be busier than now.
You're not doing enough. You should
be doing more.
You're not enough.

It's like a monster
waiting at the edge of your bed,
hoping that your foot will
d
    a
        n
            g
                l
                    e
there so that it can grab at it
and suck you into the endless abyss
underneath your bed, disappearing
in the night sky, never
returning again and leaving behind
a mystery bigger than your eaten foot.

You're far behind in life.

    You should be further.

What is wrong with you?

Something's hidden within me
that ain't transparent and wants

to be known like a self-absorbed singer.
Sometimes, it lies at the back of my ear
as it whispers to me
as I lay in the darkness of my bedroom,
trying to be responsible
and get a good night's sleep,
but it lingers and demands
me to be awake to entertain it.

appreciate the little things (ii)

Waking up.

Breathing every breath that isn't strained
in a country I sometimes don't feel I belong in.

The Bible.

Arriving at school on time
after stuffing my mouth with food
because I underestimated how long
it would take me to make breakfast,
eat, and pack my bag.

The sun beating down on me
while I cut through the air.

Four seasons.

The fresh wind.

Sitting in a packed bus.

Getting my package
after waiting 2 business weeks.

My book releasing.

My white pants and sweater are still stainless.

A matching outfit.

Food lingering in the kitchen,
begging me to eat it.

Roads without traffic jams or rush hour.

The bus speeding down the road
while the wind whips through the open windows.

Leaving class earlier than expected,
and arriving home earlier than expected.

Laughing with my family
as we watch a movie
in the living room
while the moon slowly begins to rise.

Hanging out with my friends,
sitting in the sun as the air
blows through us
while the summer heat is thick
between the space between us.

Being inside while the rain pours down.

Music.

Arriving at the bus stop
30 seconds to a minute before it arrives.

Having a seat to yourself on the bus.

Finishing writing a poetry collection.

Waking up.

two homes

The blue skies and the sunny fields light up the houses around it.

Children smile.

The air is scented differently.

The breeze dances differently.

The shadows are melting.

The rays are burning.

The shelters are crumbling like the fog down the street.

I'm afraid that people would think that I'm an alien in both of my countries.

The scent dances in the air.

My accent makes me an "other" in the countries that I call my home.

What am I supposed to do when I want to belong, but the places I'm supposed to belong to casts me out because I'm not a copied and pasted version of them?

The air is constantly thin.

It's like I'm on trial for something I didn't do because, according to them, "all Black people look the same," even though the Black woman down the street is darker than me with a freshly dark purple weave who stands three inches taller than me and whose noise points to the sky while mines point down like it hates what it smells.

I don't fit in here, and it's as if I must stand on eggshells while sitting in my home because there's always a small chance that I would get gunned down because I'm "just" another Black person.

I don't fit in there because I've been "abroad for too long," and some may dare to say I've been white-washed like the wall out there or the people who've enslaved other Black people in our history.

My culture has always walked inside of me, forming who I am like baby plants as they twist and turn around the house they decided to make their home.

I'm not white-washed.

The blue skies dance in both my homes.

The sparkles of the moon shimmer its rays.

I belong to both of my homes.

The shadows stop melting, even though I think it's only for a moment.

The birds rest in their homes.

The tree branches sway at the dust as the dust shivers from the wind that moves them like poetry that moves the hearts of the broken-hearted.

I belong here, too, you know?

My house shouldn't be stripped away like what people would do before bed just because I look or sound different.

The breeze dances differently here.

The air isn't thinning as much anymore.

My homes are my homes, and no one can take that away from me.

the monster.

It restricts my movement,
but every bit of my body moves,
my bones aching whenever I do so.
My heart strains at every beat,
begging my skin
to put it out of its misery.
Meanwhile, my skin has strained
breaths whenever I make a tiny
movement, as if my skin
wants me to melt into the couch,
        mummifying
like those mummies on TV.

The monster.

It leaks out from my dark brown eyes,
drying on my cheeks like the rain
drying up on the sandy sidewalk
during the Caribbean winter.

                      My eyes. In the dimly lit lighting,
                              it's as if my iris orbits

in blackness, wanting
to suck people's blank stares
into outer space.

It's like a black cat
as it walks in the middle
of the night as the moon
hides behind the slightly
tinted white clouds. The cat's tail
swivels   up

as it passes the basketball court
as if   yearning
to have a community of its own.

But then, in the brightness,
as if it's like the sun
as it stands in front of the slightly

tinted grey clouds,

my eyes are dark brown, wishing
to be a shimmery hazel colour
like the girls in photos
that always float around the Internet.

My dark brown eyes flicker
around me, wanting something more.

The monster

lies outside of me
but it's somehow wrapped
around me like white rope
before it leads me to its death.
It slowly squeezes around me
as it pulls me closer to where *it*
lives because *it*
just wants to not be alone anymore.
It sucks me in
like a deep purple monster's mouth
that makes its way
into children's nightmares
before disappearing
into the orbiting black skies
with the scattered stars
and the oddly shaped moon
as they attempt to give peace
to the broken-hearted people
who cry in the night sky.

j'suis peur

de perdre mon français.

I'm scared that it'll flow
from my lips, only
to be lost in the abyss.
I'm scared that the 12 or so years
would seep out of me
and that the French alphabetical milky
orange and red soup would only be found
at the bottom, screaming out
like it's been stabbed in the chest,
scared that, with any movement,
the knife would penetrate its heart.

French. It's desperate
to be understood again
as it floats in my mind
like astronauts floating through space
while tears escape between French's hidden
cracks of its white letters
that somehow have a reflection.

J'suis peur.

French doesn't consume me
like a hot blanket anymore. I don't see
its daisies as much, and I wonder
if it's been purposely
hiding from me as it prays
for my downfall while it tries
to throw silver and gold
        daggers
at me like a machine at a carnival.
Le français n'en veut plus être
dans ma tête, car c'est terrorisé
de quoi le monstre va lui faire.

Mais j'suis peur.

French's air is swelling
like the swelling of the brain
as it slowly dies
while the person carrying the brain
sits on the window sill
as it watches
the gardener take care of the plants
in their garden as the sun peaks
through the clouds.

I'm scared

that my French will leave my body,
never to return as it decides to immigrate

to a new body while I remain
just a barely-to-remember memory
in the tiniest part of its brain.

They say language is a part of your identity.

Les personnes disent
que la langue fait partie
de votre identité. Si
c'était le cas et si
le français disparaissait
de ma vie,
il faudrait que
je disparaisse avec lui.

i want to go home,
yet here is my home also.

I cried in counselling again,
wishing I was back
in my home country,
surrounded by sun and more family
as mangoes and other fruits
would litter the country. People
would walk around the street,
greeting the citizens
with warm smiles
while going to church on Sundays
while the streets would practically be empty,
except for those churchgoers
dressed in their Sunday best.
Most stores would be closed on Sundays
while heels click and clack on the ground,
echoing in the hot skies even during the winter.

The proper beaches in my home country
lie beyond the hot sand, whispering
for us to visit them.

The sun would already be set by 4 p.m.,

like the winter in my new home. Animals
would whistle in the night
as a bus somewhere has broken down,
forcing people to walk
the rest of the way, hoping
that they can stick close to someone.
Our shoes would crunch
on the light brown gravel. The moon

would sometimes be out. The bus

would still be stuck somewhere. Some people

would already be asleep.

The country is surrounded by water.

The calming waves can be heard
whispering to the moon.

I want to be back there, laughing
with more of my family members
on the porch of a house I own.

I want the winter sun
to soak into my skin
as I sit outside while on my laptop
and greet a neighbour as they walk past
as their face droops, only
wanting to be consumed
in their bed with blankets

and pillows surrounding them
like a wall protecting its people.

I want to be home again.

the disappearance of happiness

Some mornings,
I wake up
with happiness in my hands
as it stares at me with a child-like wonder,
its mouth slightly up in a smile
before happiness surveys
my room like it has never
been there. Happiness

is a yellow ball, expecting me
to know what to do with it.
It hope that I don't put it
in my back pocket, only
to forget about it
after completing my morning routine.
But I shouldn't have or call it a routine.
What if someone kills me
over it because somehow,
they would know my every movement
as if I'm secretly under surveillance by the cops?

I lay in my bed and wondered,

Why was I happy?
as if I couldn't be happy to be happy.

The earth is quiet,
even though the morning still yearns
for me to be a part of it
as the happiness rapidly
dwindles, like my grades
in Math 8 and Math 10.

Happiness disappears,
and I look around as if expecting
it to magically appear
like in movies meant
for little children.

Happiness.

Depending on the day,
it comes back to me,
wanting me to hold it
like a baby child as they look at me
in the eyes like they trust me
with their whole world
as they coo and giggle.

Happiness may not come back
until later that week, welcoming me
with full arms like a loving parent
after not seeing their child
for two and a half weeks.

Some mornings,
I wake up earlier than usual
with sleepiness still
dwelling in my eyes,
and happiness isn't residing
deep within me. Yet sadness
isn't there either, welcoming me
with open arms. There's this numbness
that festers as if it wants something from me.

Happiness.

It always comes back to me at some point.

the fear of a broken heart

I feel like I don't know
what I'm feeling most of the time
until I'm "forced"
to unravel my feelings in counselling
as he sits at the other side of the screen
while I cry because of either
my finances or feeling like

I don't have that one person
to go to or feeling as if
      I'm alone
even though I know I ain't alone.

Maybe I've contained the sadness
behind an obsidian cage at the back of my heart
for far too long. *And even then,*
my heart's locked in a chest
that no one has dared to try to open.

My heart has felt like it's always been in this cage,
only allowing Someone in but refusing
to let other people in

even though I know I should.

The feelings are stored *somewhere*
in my body, refusing to resurface
as if I'll somehow damage them.
It's like they've wrapped
themselves there purposefully
because they don't like
the outside world
because it's "too dark and scary."

        It's as if no one has been brave enough
        to try to get to my heart or the feelings
        that somehow come with it.

        Maybe it's better to keep most people out
        as I continue to laugh and smile
        with my family and friends
        as they continue to crack jokes
        with smiles overwhelming their faces.
        At least I know I wouldn't
        get my heart broken if I kept it that way.

reasons to be happy (not an exhaustive list)

- God
- Being a child of God
- My family and friends laughing, their chest rising and falling whenever they do so as happiness is painted over their faces
- Poetry and its flow from my fingertips as my fingers run across the black keyboard of my laptop
- Publishing work (other people's works and mines)
- Utilizing the gifts God has given me
- My photography while my camera explores the world like it's its purpose
- The rain flowing even though I don't like being in the rain
- The heat piercing through my home during the summer as the coolness inside consumes me
- Writing and how it flows through my fingers
- A bed that begs for me to go to sleep and begs for me to remain in bed
- & more

the dangers of a bed

I lay on my side
while lying in my bed
as my eyes skim the screen
of my "phone." The illuminating
of the screen consumes my face
and blocks out the darkness. *Maybe
it's good that it blocks out the darkness
while subconsciously
giving me some serotonin.* The "phone"
perfectly sits in my small hands, desperate
for me to keep holding them,
afraid that something
would happen if I don't keep holding it
as if it's something precious and rare. My heart
rubs against my arm. It beats
like drums in sync with the band's bass guitar.

It *feels* as if my heart
wants to be closer and closer
to my arm. It almost
bursts out of my body
like a hot red fire hydrant shooting out water.

The white fan blasts out coldness,
and I think light goosebumps form
on my arms as if fall is quickly coming.

A high *hmm* plagues the thickness
of the air in my bedroom.

Stillness has already covered the house.

Faint echoes from construction lie
in the distance. The echoes dance in the skies,
wanting people to hear it out like an opera song.

My eyes carry their own suitcases
as they wait underneath my eyes,
but my eyes force them to stay
while making them
pack more stuff.

My room's covered in darkness
like the blackest paint in the store,
covering a bedroom dedicated
to the house owners' painting room.
The blackness wants to consume me, too.
Meanwhile, the house is coated
in silentness, and it craves
      any
form of entertainment
like a restless child or adult on the bus.

The house wants to be seen in the light,

desperate to be in the sun
and covered with its love and care.
               The house wants to be known once again
                   as if it's been starved of attention
                            since its "birth."
My bed comforts me,
even though I'm not crying tears
consumed with blue while staining my cheeks.
      And then another night
slips away from me
with another dreamless sleep.

the bloody chainsaw

Life is tinted light grey
but almost always turns darker
when the time is right.
      Life wants to grab people,
      wanting to tint the people
      in grey and have their faces
      mashed in like zombies. Their arms
      would be covered in boils
      that look like they could be infections
      that could be passed along by touch.
It reaches out, desperate
for a warm hug,
and to feel the blood pulsing
through the skin and the heart
nearly beating out of the chest,
nearly as if it wants to die, too.

Life wants to be included
in the sunshine and promises
that someone has described
what Life *should* be
rather than what Life *actually* is

and what Life *actually*
is doing, which is attempting
to chase people
around with a dark grey chainsaw,
wanting to decapitate them.

*Is Life just a constant state
of slightly grey delusion
as people say, "Life gets better"
while you're slowly getting sucked down
in Life's dark grey-tinted hole
that perfectly sits in the middle of your bedroom?*

*Is Life just a constant strain on the Earth
while pushing against people's hearts
as it whispers, "I can kill you if you so desire
and even if you don't want it"?*

*Is Life supposed to be a constant
blood-curtailing scream
as its voice is splashed
in dark red paint
while its eyes are bleeding
as if it's been shot?*

I sit at the dining room table
with my laptop shining
back at me as my right hand
rests on my black mouse
while my eyes gloss over
my marketing textbook

before taking digital notes.

My chest is heavy, almost
like it's a heavy rock
at the bottom of the ocean.

I thought Life promised me
to be the shining star. I thought
it promised me to be a yellow blanket
covering my body. I thought Life promised me
her Life.

wreckless suicide

I stand at the edge of the sidewalk
as cars zoom past me.

The bus stop stands to my right.

The sun beams onto me
like a warm mother's hug
after not seeing her child for three months.

The thinning clouds float throughout the skies.

People overwhelm the bus stop
as if they don't know how to act
even though they're adults.

At least it would be an accident.

i think ending this collection is better than killing myself

There isn't a clear end.
It's as if I'm leaving these pages
on a cliff as I hope that,
when I get back to it,
it will still be there,
waiting for me with agonizing
hands as it wants to reach out

but is scared to do so.

This end isn't like a full stop
at the end of a grammatically correct sentence
      or even a semicolon
in the middle of sentences,
as they're *desperate*
to be seen and understood because
      someone
has failed to teach people
how to properly use it.
It's like the "misunderstood" family member,
and at family gatherings,
they're isolated and seen as an outcast

because their family is too busy not
wanting to be with them
because they "don't know how to handle them,"
as if they're an inanimate object.

I don't know if this is the end. I don't know
if my cup is finished
being poured onto the carpeted
ground as it hopes
I'd be magically repaired,
but deep down, knowing
that it doesn't work that way.

But maybe this is the end.
Maybe the fact that *these* words
are flowing from my fingertips
is an indicator that the collection
is complete and that my words
can be put to rest
while somehow having readers absorb
them and craving for more.

Maybe it's better off this way,
having my things called emotions
contained in a shorter piece
rather than striving for something slightly
longer, because that means
I've been spending more of my days
     crying
in the dark, questioning
if I'd ever be enough,

if I should kill myself,
and more.
Plus, ending this collection is better than suicide.

ABOUT THE POET

Angel-Clare Linton is a poet, writer, editor, and publisher. She is also the founder of Spray Paint Magazine. You can follow her on Instagram at anglclare.linton.

MORE BOOKS BY ANGEL-CLARE LINTON

The Process: A Recovery (chapbook)
Poetry on the Bookcase (poetry collection)

www.ingramcontent.com/pod-product-compliance
Lightning Source LLC
Chambersburg PA
CBHW031120080526
44587CB00011B/1053